The Great Little EXETER Book

SEMPER FIDELIS

Chips Barber

Sally Barber

ILLUSTRATIONS:
Jane Reynolds

INTRODUCTION

The Great Little Exeter Book is written for the ordinary person in the street, visitor or local, indeed anyone who wants to know just a little more about the places and items of interest in Exeter. It is not a dedicated history book and covers no subject in any great depth, but tries to draw attention to the many fascinating features of Exeter.

The collection of beautiful drawings by Jane Reynolds covers many parts of the City and I have made a few personal observations and included a few stories and facts about each place. Over a period of years I have guided hundreds of people along the various tour routes in Exeter and I have come to the conclusion that many folk have only a scant knowledge of the things they see or walk past almost every day. In researching this little book I too discovered many things that I didn't know, and my wife admits that it has opened her eyes to the surroundings we have lived in all our lives.

The book is arranged in four sections and each could form the basis of a 'city walk'. The first chapter goes on a 'Tour of the City's Walls', a journey often only undertaken by visitors, and is followed by a casual saunter 'Around and About the Cathedral'. The 'City Centre' is the basis of the third exploration and, finally, there is a stroll 'Along the Water-front', a kingdom of many pubs (who still thinks researching is dull?)

It took a year to compile all the illustrations for this book and I would like to publicly thank Jane for producing such masterly pieces that turn this book into a perfect souvenir of Exeter, if only for the pictures!

I hope that you will enjoy this book, and read it in the same spirit in which it was written - a lighthearted, but necessarily brief, study of Devon's Mother City.

A TOUR OF THE CITY'S WALLS

There is a lot to be learnt from a tour around Exeter's old city walls. This little book tells many stories, from times both ancient and modern, to make the perambulation a more interesting and edifying experience and, hopefully, will show why the settlement was so important long ago.

The wall around Exeter is far from complete now, the demands of a modern city having made inroads into them, but sections do exist and, apart from a few busy main roads, there are many interesting things to be seen on a circumnavigation. In the past, when the wall was complete, a tour was made each year, along the ramparts, to see what repairs were necessary. This was the muraltie walk, 'mur' coming from the French word which means wall.

Whilst you walk around the wall you may well wonder how people in the past organised their toilet arrangements, as most of the houses in old Exeter lacked any sanitation at all. Water was usually acquired from the Great Conduit at the carfax at the top of Southgate Street (South Street today) or from waterbearers who delivered it for a fee. From 1508 toilet facilities were limited in Exeter to three locations near the City Wall where common latrines were available. Widraghtes or Common Jakes existed at Friernhay, Paul street and at the Watergate. Their precise location is not known - so tread carefully! For the record, the only conveniences close to the circuit of the wall today are opposite Dean Clarke House (the former R D & E Hospital) in Southernhay.

The best place to start a perambulation is at the East Gate, opposite Boots the Chemist in the High Street. There is a plaque embedded in the ground, as well as a raised stone, to indicate the location of the former East Gate. Crazy paving, towards Princesshay, marks the line of the wall but first take a look at a nearby subterranean artifact well worth exploring.

The underground passages are Exeter's most unusual attraction, often forgotten by locals, but they welcome visitors with shelter on a typical English summer afternoon (ie from rain) and also offer a cool retreat on those rare, hot sunny days.

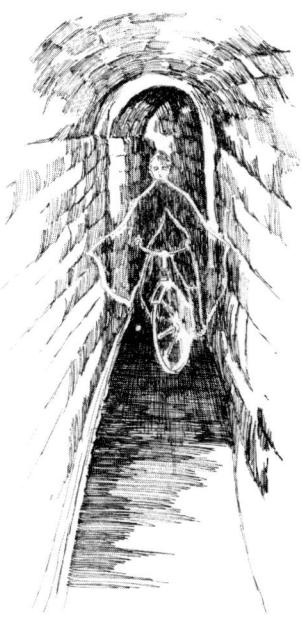

For two summers, many years ago, I worked as a guide to the underground passages, and I can thoroughly recommend a twenty-minute (or so) visit. Naturally guides have their own patter, a mixture of wit and wisdom, fact and fantasy, aimed at entertaining and interesting the visitors. But one poor guide got more than he bargained for when he saw a ghost riding through the passages on a bicycle!

The passages were built to carry water from the bountiful springs of St Sidwella, just outside the city wall, and the Cathedral Well, near Exeter City's football ground, down to the Cathedral precincts and adjacent town. The springs of the Long Brook were cleverly diverted into the passages and the water ran along using the gravity flow principle, a light gradient of less than one per cent. The floor was originally dish shaped but has been surfaced to allow visitors to proceed more comfortably. In the fourteenth century lead pipes were laid down to carry a cleaner supply, free from the dirt or sand included up to then. Experts have dated parts of the passages as being constructed in the twelfth century.

The Cathedral went to a great deal of trouble and expense to secure a regular water supply to satisfy its needs. Its own spring, near the Bishop's Palace, was irregular and unreliable. The springs were powerful and constant, although at times they caused the Cathedral folk to tangle with the local population over the right to utilise them. The local townsfolk fetched their 'passages' water at a great conduit which was located at a crossroads, the Carfax, close to the junction of North St, South St, Fore St, and High St. This conduit was taken down in 1835 as it proved to be too much of an obstacle, with its attendant queues of water consumers in the narrow South St, the main artery into Exeter.

The visitor to the passages will only see a small section of them as many are too narrow to accommodate the curious. However there is enough to see including ancient 'dipping holes'. There is an overflow passage which goes beneath the corner of Boots, but watch out for the modern pipes which form a perfect training ground for would-be limbo dancers!

The source which supplied a lot of the water to the passages was known as the springs of St Sidwella, a tragic saint who gave her name to the district.

Sidwella was a pure, devout and beautiful girl, daughter of a wealthy Romanized Briton who lived in Exeter. He died a Christian, whilst his children were still young, and left them in the custody of his second wife, the proverbial cruel stepmother. Sidwella's stepmother was jealous of her, particularly as she (Sidwella) inherited the bulk of her father's fortune. The evil stepmother plotted Sidwella's death and employed a corn reaper to murder her. Whilst Sidwella knelt in silent prayer in the fields the corn reaper cut her head off with a scythe. It is said that a gushing spring of sparkling water suddenly appeared at the spot where her head fell.

It is believed that a few centuries later her bones were buried at the Cathedral. In the East Window she is depicted with a scythe and a gushing well. She is also depicted on the front of Tesco's store in Sidwell Street, close to the location where she was slain, and from whence her springs sprung.

The wall will be seen on the far side of Post Office Street and runs beside it towards Bedford Street. The far side of the wall provides pleasanter surroundings with many benches available to rest weary limbs. For those who like to get closer to nature ...

Southernhay Green is regarded by some people as one of the most attractive features of any town in England, and indeed it has a beauty and elegance which is hard to match. The area was planned and developed in Georgian times when the city was full of prosperous merchants, all keen to build splendid town houses. The principal builders of Georgian Exeter were William Hooper and Matthew Nosworthy, the latter being responsible for many of the terrace houses in Southernhay in the period between 1795 and 1820. There are many fine Georgian buildings in and around the city centre which include Barnfield Crescent, Colleton Crescent and Dix's Field, which, incidentally was the birthplace of the writer, traveller and folk song collector, the Rev. Sabine Baring Gould, the man who popularised the song "Widecombe Fair".

Today the bulk of these Georgian buildings are used as offices, ideally located in the business centre of Exeter. Those workers who toil and sweat over endless cups of tea, may gaze out of their office windows across this elongated strip of parkland which once possessed a couple of ponds known as Crolditch. These were not landscaped to please the eye but cesspools to offend the sense of smell, the sort of place to discard the carcass of a dead horse!

Now we have a pleasant area which possesses over fifty trees, including nearly thirty different species. Among them are four Exeter Oaks which are a cross between a Cork oak and a Turkey Oak made, by accident, in the eighteenth century by an Exeter arborealist (tree expert). Perhaps the most striking tree in Southernhay is the London Plane, a majestic tree which does better than any other species in big cities, having a high pollution tolerance which (of course) is not needed in Exeter.

As the Roman wall disappears behind Fanum House, the AA Headquarters, it is necessary to walk along the first terrace of Georgian houses in Southernhay before turning right towards the Close. The bridge which spans the gap in the city wall is known as the Burnet Patch Bridge. Burnet Patch was the Mayor in 1814 and had this bridge erected so that the regular 'muraltie' inspection along the walls could be made without interruption. Next turn left and descend a flight of steps and go along the curving path beneath the wall. The Bastion which protrudes from the wall is Lollard's Tower named after the supporters of John Wycliffe, a dissident fourteenth century priest. This tower, which had deteriorated greatly, was rebuilt in 1912.

At the bottom of Southernhay is an area known as

Trinity Green. There was a graveyard in the vicinity of the public conveniences here which received many of the victims of the 1832 cholera epi-

demic. The nursing bill
for the epidemic cost the
city £270.8s.6d. It is
thought that the cholera
was brought to Exeter from
Plymouth or Weymouth, and
the Exeter doctors had to
work night and day to
fight it, ably assisted by
the nurses who had rallied
round from all parts of
the city. The doctors were
publicly thanked by the
city coucil but the nurses
had to fight for the
'liberal remuneration'
with which they had been
tempted.

Continuing along the
line of the wall, where
South Street cuts across,
was the site of the once
celebrated South Gate. This was also known as 'The Great Gate' and for many
centuries formed the main entrance to Exeter. Into its masonry fabric was
included a prison, once deemed to be the foulest hole in England. Neverthe-

less its passing in 1819 was
lamented; it was a gateway
through which numerous Kings
passed, including William the
Conqueror. It was regarded as
one of the grandest edifices in
medieval Exeter.

Today it hard to imagine that
the White Hart, an ancient inn,
now sited almost right in the
middle of the city centre, would
once have been one of the first
buildings encountered by way-
farers arriving in the city.
Once known as The Blue Boar, it
was built by William Wynard as a
private residence, complete with
its own well. The well, despite
its usefulness, was also the
cause of several tragedies; a
carpenter collapsed and died at
the bottom of it and the person
who went to his aid also died,
both apparently poisoned by a
pocket of carbonic acid gas.

The inn became The White Hart,
the favourite badge of Richard
III, and was well sited to cater

for the needs of weary travellers, or teams of packhorses, entering Exeter
through the enormous South Gate. The rear of the inn, a cobbled yard, was a

hive of activity with ostlers, saddlers, blacksmiths and other ancilleries, coping with the transport needs and demands of the day. This has given way to the sound of the motor car, visitors today being treated to a far higher standard of accommodation and fayre than their forerunners!

To get from the South Gate to the Quay there are two routes. One crosses at the top of the inner by-pass and descends Quay Lane beside the wall or the other continues to the dip in South Street and turns left into Coombe Street. This road, the route of a former stream, goes though a subway and on to Quay Hill. A right turn leads into the lane which goes behind the Custom House and beneath the Wall. This occasionally overgrown and often muddy lane was once a more residential thoroughfare and is called Cricklepit Lane.

On the left is one of the many leats which were cut through, from medieval times onwards, this part of lower Exeter, a network of watercourses providing the necessary impetus for more than twenty waterwheels. Along the lane and behind corrugated fencing are the remains of Cricklepit Mill. These mills were started in about 1194 and their name probably derives from an old Celtic word ('Creic' meaning the pit or hollow beneath the cliffs) and before the wall was built this was certainly beneath one.

The lane climbs gently with a pub on the left. This was originally The Bishop Blaize, named after the patron saint of the wool trade. Long ago there were some unusual weighing competitions in this pub involving the landlord's wife. I can divulge no more in case any under-18's are reading this!

By ascending the steps, the ever-busy inner by-pass will need to be crossed to reach one of Exeter's most attractive corners.

Just a stone's throw from the continuous noise of traffic wending its way wearily over Exe Bridges, is a corner of Exeter which is steeped in history.

Whenever I take people around the City Walls I always contrive to arrive below the 'Matthew the Miller' clock in good time to see the figures on the clock perform their 'on the hour' routine. This clock, on the church of St

Mary Steps, has a central figure, believed to be Henry VIII, and two attendant men-at-arms. Alternatively, a more romantic story abounds which claims that this is in fact the Matthew the Miller who worked at nearby Cricklepit Mill. In days when clocks were rare, Matthew lived his day-to-day life with clockwork regularity so that neighbours used him as a living timepiece. When

Matthew died it is thought that the clock was put up in his memory, and also presumably as a compensation for their loss! The clock was made by Matthew Hopping, which might suggest yet another theory?

Opposite is another famous Exeter landmark, the House that Moved. In 1961, to give better access to Exe Bridges, road improvements were undertaken and a dingy thoroughfare called Frog Street disappeared. But there was a house that was deemed worthwhile to save and restore, so it was shored up, jacked up and then hauled up to its present position on the corner of West St. It's an early fifteenth century house and replaces one of a similar nature which was on the site before. It has housed various modern business ventures that have also endured fluctuating fortunes.

The West Gate stood here until 1815 and, by all accounts, it was a poor affair and well worthy of demolition. A route across the River Exe led through this gate, and up the once important corridor of Stepcote Hill, to the town centre. William, Prince of Orange, who landed at Brixham in November 1688, marched with his army through this gate (and he didn't think much of it either!)

Stepcote Hill has over 100 steps on each side which are for pedestrians. The narrow cobbled roadway in the middle was intended for packhorses. It's believed that its name derives from an old English word meaning steep rather than from step.

9

This part of Exeter is often referred to as the West Quarter. Opinions and memories are divided between those who portray its past image as being tough, rough and seemy, and those who claim it was never that bad. Today it is an area which is undergoing a transformation and, far from being the worst area in the city, is rapidly becoming one of the best. Once, in this vicinity there was a squalid network of poorly appointed houses, depressing tenements and dark courtyards. Many of the residents derived a meagre living by working in the soap, leather or brush factories which were not far from where British Telecom has its Exe Bridges headquarters today. However, there are many former residents of this district who are very proud of their association with the West Quarter and who will paint an altogether different picture of conditions and life styles (and have done so already, so please don't write to tell me again!) of those good old, bad old days.

West Street is quite a steep climb but beyond the junction with Fore Street and New Bridge Street the going along Bartholomew Street is much easier.

Stepcote Hill

Barts Tavern takes its name directly from Bartholomew Street. For a while it changed its name to The Merry Monk but soon 'kicked the habit' to return to its original name. Although the tavern is in an old building, this is deceptive because it has only been a pub for about forty years; it was originally built as a warehouse, being one of many in this area.

There is a beautiful chapel on the bend in Bartholomew Street which was built in 1818 to seat between 800-1,000 Baptist worshippers. During the last war it was used for the war effort and has also been used as a school and a store.

By not following the road around the sharp bend to the right, but proceeding past the railings beside the left hand side of the chapel and along the line of the city wall, reveals a fine view, evidence that the site of Exeter was an excellent one on which to develop an important town. The steep slopes made it easy to defend and the raised situation of the city gave good views in most directions. From this point Exwick, Redhills, the Haldon Hills and the distant estuary are clearly visible.

The sharp bend in the path is known as Snayle Tower, the former location of one of the 'common jakes', an early form of public convenience. The tower in this place name certainly existed, according to city records, in 1437 and was possibly so named because of its odd shape and colour. There are no visible remains today.

Beyond the steep Barbican Steps, which lead down to Exe Street, is the church yard of Allhallows-on-the-Walls, a Church which has been demolished.

This area was the first to be settled and a small settlement even existed here before the Romans arrived. The district acquired the name 'Little Britayne' because it was occupied by the British in Saxon times.

Beneath this graveyard on the side of the hill are some cavernous constructions which may be reached by descending a narrow flight of twisting steps.

Catacombs are underground galleries with niches for tombs (or so says my trusty dictionary). In this case Exeter's catacombs are built against the wall and are thus not strictly subterranean vaults, even though they are pretty gloomy, dank and damp. They consist of a long central arched passage with recesses on each side. These were originally intended to be honeycombed but only one was completed like this. Each cell was to be a little larger than a coffin with two holes in the roof to enable the wooden overcoats to be lowered from street level. Once in position this cell was sealed with a single stone slab bearing the name, age and birthplace of the deceased. The earliest recorded burial in these catacombs was in 1811 whilst the last was about 1883. Anglicans were buried to the right of the gate whilst others went to the left. Presumably it was believed there would be similar arrangements in Heaven!

The catacombs, as a financial venture, were a disaster - only fifteen people were buried there and only three of them were Anglicans.

There was a store located in one of the recesses for burning the clothes of cholera victims, from the 1832 outbreak, and later another part of the catacombs was separated off by a brick partion and used as the City Mortuary - making this, perhaps, the dead centre of Exeter?

Beyond the line of railings above the catacombs is an unusual looking building for this part of the world, a malthouse. Malt was made here for a nearby brewery at a time when Exeter had thirty working breweries. Today there are none and this malthouse has been converted into a restaurant.

An old malthouse

On the next junction, at the bottom of North Street, is the entrance to the city from the north across the deep depression of the Long Brook. Opposite the North Gate commemorative stone is the Crown and Sceptre Inn, an old coaching house which was built in 1769 co-inciding with a new six-horse coach service to Barnstaple - one of the few routes left in Britain where motorists doing the same journey today will see little improvement in the travel conditions!

The Iron Bridge is an unusually large piece of antique ironware which spans the valley of the Long Brook, a stream that now runs well below the surface down to the river near the Mill on the Exe. It is often referred to as North Bridge for the entrance to the city, through the North Gate, was along this alignment.

One of the more unusual items to be discovered on a tour of the walls is here at the North Gate, at the top of a very long pole. Looking skyward will reveal an unusual weather vane, or is it a weather dragon? It is ornamented in gold foil and was re-erected by the Exeter Civic Society. Seen in some lights, small dimples may be observed. These are believed to be bullet marks made during the English Civil War (1642-1646).

The North Gate was the first of the original four gates to be removed in 1769; in those days redevelopment was a much slower process and it took fifty years to demolish the last one, the South Gate, in 1819. The Iron Bridge arrived in 1835 after the valley bottom had been filled up, thereby making the piles less difficult to sink.

The bridge was built by Russell and Brown of Worcester at a cost of £9,000. The units required in its construction were so big that they had to be brought by sea, the railway to Exeter not yet having arrived (not BR's fault this time - the railway lines hadn't actually been laid!) There was as much protest against it being built then, as there would be today if they threatened to demolish it.

Naturally the bridge was constructed to take less demanding weights than today's traffic, and there have been various schemes, including the strategically placed bollards, to restrict misuse of the bridge. If you look closely you may notice that some of the kerbstones display a well worn edge, a result of carriage drivers deliberately using them to brake against. The bridge has also been something of a death trap and many travellers have succumbed to its perils.

The area around it is full of interest and some unusual shops and businesses continue to trade in the shadow of the neighbouring complex of city centre shops. Like its near neighbour, the West Quarter, this part of Exeter is also enjoying a rebirth.

By descending the steps, near the North Gate, Northernhay Street will provide a quieter backwater route than Paul Street, up to Queen Street. The wall will appear high at this point but is dwarfed by a modern shopping complex.

On the far side of Queen Street the hustle and bustle of city noise and traffic can easily be forgotten.

Within a few minutes walk of Exeter's city centre there are two adjacent public open spaces - Rougemont Gardens and Northernhay Park - which have much to commend them, although the painful ravages of graffiti 'artists' and mindless vandals have made their ugly presence felt on what should be a wonderful retreat for peace and quiet.

The gardens have a history and it has been claimed that Northernhay is the oldest public park in England. It was originally laid out in 1612 with many shaded avenues of trees. Alas, the number of trees has dwindled considerably and the secluded nature of the park has given way to a more open prospect, with views across the northern and western sides of the city.

Despite losing its avenues of trees there is still much to attract the ornamental gardener with a fine array of shrubs, many of them rare. The local firm of Veitch, which has been established for well over a century,

14

made a world wide search for suitable plants for the park in the period between 1840 and 1905. One plant, Eucryptia Glutinosa, was acquired by Veitch from Chile in 1859, and is still thriving in the park, just one of over 400 species which can be seen.

In the early part of this century regimental and city bands performed there three nights a week in summer, and touring bands also appeared when visiting the city. Also Exeter's annual flower show was held there.

There are many memorials within the grounds, the main target of the vandal. Poor Thomas Dyke Acland, whose statue stands perilously close to the ramparts on the city wall, has endured cruel tortures and various parts of his anatomy have been removed at times - and storm damage in 1980 didn't do him much good either!

At the top of the slope rising up from Queen Street, is a memorial to the dead of the First World War. It is regarded as one of the finest of its type in the country, and around its base will be seen four bronze figures of war, a soldier, a sailor, a prisoner of war and a nurse. Atop the memorial is depicted

the main bronze Figure of Victory which is trampling over the Demon of Tyranny and Wrong. It is the work of a local man, John Angel, and is a fitting reminder of those 958 men from Exeter who died between 1914-1918.

The leisurely stroller through the gardens will notice a tall slender tower protruding upwards from the wall. This is Athelstan's tower which can be inspected more closely as a path passes through it. Athelstan was the grandson of King Alfred and was responsible, in the tenth century, for strengthening the city defences. He had a dyke created at Barnfield, just beyond the walls on the opposite side of the city, which is still known as Athelstan's Dyke, and a nearby road is called Athelstan Road. It is believed that Athelstan also had a palace in Paul Street where Habitat now stands (although it is doubtful whether it was as well furnished as today's trendy store). Athelstan also founded the monastery of St Mary and St Peter where the Cathedral now stands.

At the other end of Northernhay Gardens, near the exit into Northernhay Place, is a fine Bronze statue called 'The Deerstalker' by Stephens. He also made the statue of Thomas Dyke Acland (1861) and that of Prince Albert (1870) which stands on the museums in Queen Street. At a banquet, to commemorate the unveiling of The Deerstalker, he made a very modest speech thanking his patrons and best friends with the promise that he wanted to represent "that which is true and to do that which is right". When The Deerstalker was first erected it stood in Bedford Circus but was later removed to its present position.

Just past this statue are the exit gates of Northernhay Park and a gentle stroll down Northernhay Place returns us to the High Street and Eastgate where we began. Anyone for a lap of honour?

AROUND AND ABOUT THE CATHEDRAL

When writing about Exeter's great and glorious Cathedral, it is always difficult to know exactly what to put in and what to leave out. The true historian describes it with a procession of dates and details, often so obscure that the 'ordinary' reader rapidly turns the page in search of something more readily digestable. It is possible to obtain a fuller historical inventory of all the amazing artefacts and occurrences of this highly regarded building and the enthusiast should also go on a guided tour. This short piece merely aspires to whet the appetite and to serve as a reminder of the experience.

The first church on the site was built in Saxon times and only lasted seventy years. William Warelwast, a nephew of William the Conqueror, replaced it with a nobler building in Norman style. The twin towers still remain and are distinctive landmarks which can be seen from many miles around the local countryside. The north tower is St Paul's and its twin, the south tower, is St John's.

Through the medieval period changes occurred gradually, shaping today's appearance of the Cathedral. The great east window dates back to 1391 but some of its glass is even older than that. The minstrels' gallery is a fine example of fourteenth century craftsmanship built when Bishop Grandisson was fashioning his changes. Sculptured in the front are many medieval musical instruments which include a cittern, bagpipes, clarion, rebec, psaltery, syrinx, sackbut, regals, gittern, shalm, timbrel, and cymbals - all harmoniously portrayed (and all correctly spelt!)

On a different note, in the North Transept, is a quaint old clock. Peter Lightfoot, a Monk of Glastonbury, reputedly made similar clocks for Wimborne Minster, Ottery St Mary, and Wells Cathedral, but if the date of 1480 is correct, then Lightfoot could not have made this one as he was already dead then! The clock shows the hour of the day and the age of the moon. Upon its dial are two circles, representing the days and the hours. In the centre is a semi-globe, the Earth, around which a half gold, half black moon revolves every month. Between the two circles is a third ball which represents the sun which points, with a fleur-de-lys, to the hours. (In medieval times it was believed that the sun travelled around the Earth every day - oh how the years rush by!) Referring to the hours of the day, the Latin inscription Pereunt et imputantur means "They pass and are placed to our account". In 1760 an additional dial was made to show minutes.

The hours are struck by the Great Peter Bell which weighs more than four tons and is the second biggest bell in England. It is therefore not surprising that it is only struck and not swung! It is usually called The Peter and was presented by Archdeacon Peter Courtenay in 1484.

The miserichords, some forty-nine in number, are probably the oldest in England. On one of them is a carving known as the Exeter Elephant which was created by a craftsman who only had a verbal description to go on as to what such a creature might look like. Consequently he created a splendid, but somewhat unusual, beast with hoofs and hind legs just like a horse! The carving was prompted by Bishop William Brewer who journeyed around the known world in the thirteenth century. You will find it in the choir of the Cathedral, under the seat of the sixth stall on the left-hand side as you face the altar.

The Cathedral was thoroughly restored between 1870-1877 under the watchful eye of Sir Gilbert Scott.

A tour of the Cathedral is not just an appreciation of its architecture, but a living history lesson with so much to read or interpret from the walls and windows. The names which appear evoke great memories of times of war and peace, tragedy and triumph, and many tell a tale to animate this incredible edifice. There is a window to the memory of Richard Blackmore, author of the celebrated Exmoor saga 'Lorna Doone' which is, ironically, based on a Dartmoor story. There is another one in memory of William Reginald, 'The Good', eleventh Earl of Devon. And perhaps on a more down to 'earth' level, a brass recording the generosity of Mr Willey who presented the Electric Installation to the Cathedral in 1904.

Our brief appraisal of Exeter Cathedral will end on a technical note, for it is interesting to note the vital statistics of the cathedral. Externally it is 409 feet long, the nave and aisles are 72 feet wide, the height of the vaulting above the floor is 68 feet whilst the transept has a length of 138 feet. Finally, those twin towers which dominate the skyline stand a proud 130 feet above the surrounding ground.

The area of the Cathedral Close and Yard is the spiritual heart of Exeter, an almost triangular shaped area which attracts many thousands of visitors each year, but is still a relatively quiet retreat. The Close was probably more aptly named in the past when no less than seven gates controlled entry to it. In 1285 Walter Lechlade, the Precentor of the Cathedral, was murdered in the early hours of the morning (the first service was held about two o'clock) and his murderer escaped through the South Gate. It had not been closed, either by design or by accident, and the King ordered both the

Mayor, Alfred Duport, and the porter of the Gate, to be executed for negligence. The Close was walled in 1286, with the consent of King Edward, and the gates were closed each night when the Cathedral curfew bell was rung so that no unauthorised person could enter.

One gate was sited opposite the Episcopal Palace, whilst Broadgate (sometimes known as St Michael's gate) opened to the High Street. St Martins Lane provided a third entrance, whilst the main pack horse route towards the Cathedral precincts was through the Beargate. Pedestrians favoured a little wicket gate entrance called Little Style, which was located on the western side of the Close opening towards South Street. Another route lay through the Bickleigh Gate by St Catherine's Chapel, now a heap of ruins between Bedford Street and The Close, named after the Bickleigh family whose residence was close by.

The seventh entrance was via a church and was called the Gate of St Petrock. St Petrock was a Celt, descended from a noble family, who entered a monastery

and then went on a mission to Ireland. His Celtic wanderings brought him back to Devon and Cornwall and then on to a pilgrimage to Jerusalem and Rome. He saw out his days as Prior of Bodmin, passing away at the age of ninety in 564 AD. Many churches are named after this celebrated local saint who bore the title Apostle of the West. It is believed that the peal of bells at St Petrock are the lightest in England, a stark contrast to those of the nearby Cathedral, which are the heaviest in the land, two extremes almost side by side.

In the past anyone wishing to trade within this confined area had to seek permission from the Bishop.

According to the local street directory for Exeter, the Cathedral Yard stretches from the Royal Clarence Hotel to Three Gables, where Webb and Bower have their gift shop, and the Cathedral Close runs from St Martins Church, beside Mol's, to Southernhay and then back to Palace Gate, the other two sides of this triangular area.

The Cathedral Green lies within the triangle, and is a popular place for shop and office workers to repose at lunch times. The majority will be blissfully unaware that where their weary bones rest, there once rested many old worn out bones as this was a cemetery. Bartholomew's cemetery on the city walls had to be opened because this one by the Cathedral was filled to overflowing. A grave situation indeed.

The white statue of Richard Hooker enjoys a privileged position on Exeter's hallowed Cathedral Green. The statue endures the full rigours of the weather and everything that the resident pigeons care to throw at it. This could be considered a further test of this great man's qualities for when he lived, 1554-1600, he was regarded as divine for his meekness, modesty, temperance and virtue. He wrote many books on the history of religious thought, including his masterpiece "Of the Laws of Ecclesiastical Polity", published in 1594. His writings meant so much to him that as he lay on his death bed, on discovering that his house had been broken into, his only question was, "Are my books safe?"

He made the unfortunate mistake of marrying the daughter of a lady who had nursed him when he was ill. His wife gave him a hard time and it was widely known that he was very unhappy about his domestic situation. Izaak Walton described Hooker's wife as an ill-bred, bad-tempered girl. On a journey from London to Gravesend Hooker caught a fatal cold. It is said that his wife remarried immediately, only to die within a month or two of Hooker. Through his works he did much to establish the Anglican Church on a sure foundation.

The statue is the work of Mr Alfred Drury and was presented to the City in 1907.

There is much to see on a stroll around the Cathedral Yard and Close. Here are a few more of its treasures to contemplate and enjoy.

Mol's Coffee House is not a coffee house in the true sense and appears never to have been one! However it is strongly believed that it was a subscription coffee house for well over a century from about 1700-1824. Mol was not a gangster's girlfriend - he was Thomas Mol, an Italian, who was at these premises in 1596, many decades before coffee was even introduced into England.

It has also been suggested that this was a favourite and frequent rendezvous location for Devon's famous sea dogs when plotting to thwart the

Mol's Coffee House

Spanish Armada. It is believed that the famous seamen to meet there included Hawkins, Grenville, Frobisher and the legendary Sir Francis Drake. This was obviously more of a club for the elite rather than just a place of refreshment open to all.

The building contains one of the finest oak panelled rooms in the country; it has a star shaped ceiling, believed to be the only one of its kind in Europe. There are 230 panes of glass and not one of them is a perfect square.

The site has been used for many purposes. An earlier house, in the sixteenth century, was used by the clergy whose survival depended on benefactors and legacies. The idea was that the priests would pray for the souls of those who endowed them.

By the end of the nineteenth century Mol's had become Worth's Art Gallery with the distinctive Dutch Gable and an extra floor added to make it resemble the building we see today. It remains one of the most photographed landmarks in Exeter.

From Mol's, where great seamen may or may not have plotted outstanding deeds, the Cathedral Close gently ebbs away towards more peaceful pursuits. There are many business enterprises which quietly go about their workaday tasks behind the facade of ancient buildings.

Further along at No 7 Cathedral Yard stands the premises of the Devon and Exeter Institute which was set up to promote the advancement of Science, Literature and the Arts. The building is said to have originally been one of the Tudor gatehouses and was also the town house of the Courtenays, the Earls of Devon.

The Bishop's Palace lies behind the Chapter House. Its impressive Cathedral Library contains "The Exeter Book" (Codex Exoniensis) the largest anthology of Anglo-Saxon poems in existence. It was given by Leofric when the See was transferred from Crediton to Exeter in 1050.

When the Royal Clarence, a fine Georgian building, opened for trade in 1769 it was simply called The Hotel - a unique title at the time for it was the first establishment in England to utilise this French term. Its landlord

was a Frenchman, Pierre Berlon, which may explain why. It acquired its present name after the Duchess of Clarence, later Queen Adelaide of England, wife of William IV, stayed at the hotel on two occasions. There have been many other distinguished visitors including Lord Nelson in 1801 and the Duke of Kent, father of Queen Victoria. Not that he would have paid much attention to his surroundings on his last visit as he was dead when he arrived! He had been visiting Sidmouth but died there in January 1820 and was brought back to repose at the Hotel whilst arrangements were made to convey his body back to London.

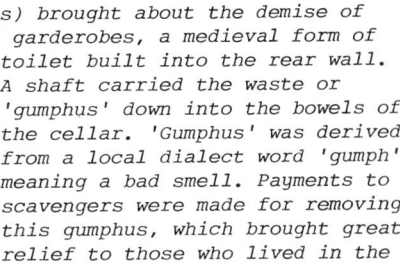

It has been said that you cannot be arrested by the police for being drunk and disorderly either in or outside of the Clarence, as it is ecclesiastical territory and certain offences like this are above the law. However, the landlord must away to the Cathedral and summon the verger - and he will arrest you!

A recent addition to The Royal Clarence is The Well House which occupies the site of a former bookshop. Beneath ground floor level is one of many wells found in the vicinity. Roman coins and pottery have been unearthed from here in the past. The well is about thirty feet deep and built of local stone, probably hewn from Northernhay.

The SPCK Bookshop at the Cathedral end of Martins Lane is housed in a building which is more than 500 years old. It has been a bookshop since 1961 and attracts a vast number of visitors through its doors each year.

The bookshop consists of a pair of three-storeyed houses made into one by the removal of the oak screen which originally separated them. They were constructed in timber framing supported by a red sandstone rear wall. The stone was hewn from the ancient quarries of Wonford about one and a half miles away. Originally there were four houses in a row but an extension to the nearby premises of Dingles (then Colsons) brought about the demise of the other two. Each of the houses contained garderobes, a medieval form of

toilet built into the rear wall. A shaft carried the waste or 'gumphus' down into the bowels of the cellar. 'Gumphus' was derived from a local dialect word 'gumph' meaning a bad smell. Payments to scavengers were made for removing this gumphus, which brought great relief to those who lived in the lower levels of the houses!

The SPCK building has had many uses. It has been a home for priests, craftsmen and tradesmen. Many businesses have been conducted from it including a boot and shoe maker, a tailor, umbrella maker, a hairdresser in 1878, a tobacconist and hairdresser in 1890, a second-hand bookshop, an antique shop and a Cathedral Art Gallery. Other parts of the same building have been used by a German yeast dealer and a watch maker - who bided his time here for many years.

Tinley's stands beside the former Broadgate (the main gate into the walled Cathedral Close). The gate was a restriction to traffic and was pulled down in 1824, a fact which was cheered by the newspapers of the day but would, no doubt, produce a different response today.

Tinley's tea rooms enjoy the reputation of being the oldest and one of the finest places of refreshment in Exeter. Many famous people have taken tea there, a list which includes Leslie Crowther, Mick Jagger and The Beatles! The building has a Victorian exterior but inside an old Tudor edifice presents itself and there is evidence that it has been modified on at least four occasions. Although originally it was a hostel for travelling priests, its main use through the centuries has been as a tea room. A company called Tinley's arrived in 1932 and stayed just sixteen years - but the name stuck. A fire, which started in Chalks Store in the High Street, in 1975 threatened to destroy this ancient building. But between the rear of the High Street shops and Tinley's are the remains of the wall that abutted on The Broadgate - the only remnants of the walled Cathedral precincts - and it is this stout wall which probably saved the cafe. Another survivor of the conflagration is Fred, the resident ghost. Occasionally seen in sandals, the presence of this friendly spirit is often felt at night. He is prone to move things about and footsteps are often heard. However, he should know by now that they don't serve spirits in a tea room!

The Three Gables are tucked away to the side of St Mary Major Green near the war memorial. (St Mary Major Church was in front of the Cathedral but was demolished some years ago.) This trio of houses was built in the sixteenth century and was occupied by craftsmen attached to the Cathedral. On the building is an attractive insurance plaque of the West of England company. Solicitors now operate from here and Webb and Bower have a shop in the end property.

The granite war memorial is the work of Edwin Lutyens, famed for his work on Castle Drogo and Lindisfarne Castle. He also designed the Drum Inn at Cockington, showing his versatility as an architect.

THE CITY CENTRE

Exeter's population is around 96,000 but, as a shopping centre, it serves an area encompassing about a quarter of a million inhabitants. The natural routeways across South West England gravitate towards Exeter and so the town has grown as a regional centre. The heart of the city is a mixture of old and new shops, a vast range of business enterprises and many age old buildings. This chapter aims to convey a little of the character of central Exeter and includes some obvious and some lesser-known aspects.

The most notable and celebrated building in the High Street is the Guildhall. After a brief look at this ancient municipal building, we can radiate away along other avenues to explore the parts of the city that are just as interesting but not so famous.

Exeter's celebrated Guildhall is a magnificent place. Like so many attractions in Exeter, a vast proportion of the local population have never entered its enormous doorway to see within this treasure house - it is left mainly for visitors to enjoy.

Much of the present structure of the building dates back to about 1330, although it is certain that a civic building existed on the site many centuries earlier. In the fifteenth century, during renovation, the hall was virtually rebuilt, and the single-span timbered roof, which forms such an attractive feature, was installed about 1468. The timber was taken from Duryard, a massive wood which once clothed the hills to the north of Exeter, and is now partly covered by the University campus. Stone was brought around the coast from the Isle of Purbeck and from Beer. This was supplemented by volcanic rock from Peamore, on the edge of the present city, and from Northernhay a few hundred yards away.

The sombre day-to-day atmosphere of this chamber hides the merriment and joviality it had in former times when the king or queen's players entertained vociferous audiences with their music. It is as a venue for pageantry that it is renowned. Many ceremonies have either begun or ended there, and the list of visiting Royals and other dignitaries would be exhaustive to record. It is a place of the people, the very good and the very bad. Many men and women have been sentenced to death there and various prostitutes have been put in the stocks outside to endure public shame and the odd rotten egg (in the past, I hasten to add!)

It is regarded as the oldest municipal building in the kingdom, the earliest reference appearing in a deed of 1160. The Tudor front which straddles the High Street pavement was completed in 1593. The windows around the Guildhall contain some famous, almost legendary names, from the city's past. Recorded for posterity and perusal are the names of past Mayors, Town Clerks, Recorders and Sheriffs. There is an extremely fine painting of Princess Henrietta, daughter of Charles I. The portrait, by Sir Peter Lely, was given to the City by Charles II as a special mark of favour. The princess was born in Exeter at Bedford House in Exeter, a building which has long since gone, in a road called Bedford Circus which was a victim of the Blitz and replanning.

The Guildhall houses many civic treasures and is thus also highly important as a shrine of local history. Don't be one of those who pass by it daily and have never been in - make the effort to visit it at least once!

Charles Dickens was a regular visitor to The Turks Head and it is believed that he discovered one of his characters, the Fat Boy in 'Pickwick', here. Dickens' first visit to Exeter was probably in 1835 to report on an election for the Morning Chronicle. He leased Mile End Cotttage in the village of Alphington, three miles from the city centre, which his parents used and he visited them there often during their three and a half year stay. A plaque on the wall of the cottage commemorates this fact. Other characters created in Exeter include Mrs Lupin from Martin Chuzzlewit and Pecksniff, who was based on a local dignatory and heavily caricatured by Dickens. The Turks Head has named a dining room in his honour - the Pickwick Grill.

The name of the pub is said to derive from an unfortunate Turkish prisoner held there, at a time when that part of the building was used as a prison, who was rendered some eight inches shorter when his head was lopped off by an executioner.

When walking along Exeter's High Street it is well worth lifting your eyes above street level, for there are many unusual old frontages and facades to see, all different in style and character.

Near the entrance to Martin's Lane is a former Elizabethan House which dates back to 1564. Many Exonians will recall it as a chemist shop, renowned for being the foremost stockist of photographic equipment, and at one time there was even a dark room freely available to the public. It has since become a clothes shop.

Just above the junction with Queen Street was the venue for the cruel spectacle of bull baiting, an activity which involved ferocious dogs attacking a bull tied to a stake unable to defend itself as its horns were guarded. Now the same location is favoured by buskers who bring a much more innocent form of entertainment to the street scene.

At one time people joked that in the time it took to drive from one end of the city to the other, via Fore Street and the High Street, you could grow a beard! Exeter's High Steet has now rid itself of a high proportion of traffic by restricting access to just buses and essential vehicles. The inner and outer by-passes and the motorway have negated the need to pass through the city centre. The reduced traffic flow creates a much safer and more pleasant atmosphere for browsing, shopping and socialising.

The High Street beyond Dingles is a wider thoroughfare than existed in pre-war days. Exeter's heart was ripped out in a series of devestating raids which razed that part of the High Street to the ground, and most of the immediate area to its east. Its previous width was very much in accord with that of the lower part of the High Steet as it is seen today. Exeter was bombed as a direct reprisal for attacks made by the RAF on the historic city of Lubeck in Germany. The re-building programme has thrown up great controversy and almost every new construction has been met with much criticism.

The two impressive frontages beside C & A's store are merely a facade, the buildings behind being much altered and modern. Originally these were merchant's houses, the homes of the most influential men in a prosperous Exeter. Austin Reed's premises were restored in 1878 by Mr Lidstone of Dartmouth. For years they were used as judges' lodgings by visiting circuit judges attending the Exeter Assizes.

A little further along the High Street, the last of the pre-war buildings is on a site which once housed the official residence of the Mayor of Exeter. A plaque on an outside wall reveals that Thomas Bodley, founder of the world famous Bodleian Library, was born here on 2 March 1545. Prior to being a clothes shop it was a Lyons cafe, and before that it was the offices

of the Devon and Exeter Gazette. This location must have been good for
newspapers as the Express and Echo also had their headquarters just a few
doors away before moving to Sidwell Street.

The remainder of the High Street is post war - an urban shopping thoroughfare made interesting with a vast number of flower baskets and troughs.

Queen Street is the straightest road in Exeter and is named after Queen
Victoria. Apart from the Victorian architecture visible in many of the
buildings, there are other links with this great lady; the museum is the
Royal Albert, named in honour of her husband, and many of the past buildings
also had a connection in name with her. The Victoria Hall, which stood
almost opposite Central Station, was a small version of the Albert Hall in
London but sadly was destroyed by fire, and there were two pubs, one called
The Victoria (then the New Victoria and now something different!) and one
called The Queen's Hotel. A statue was put up at the city end of the street
to mark her 29th birthday.

Prior to being Queen Street, part of this road was known as Market Street.
The congestion caused by traders, animals and
customers necessitated the building of
Exeter's Higher Market, the only visible
remains being the impressive series of columns
which forms an entrance to the Guildhall Shopping Centre. This market opened in July 1838
and survived until September 1962. George
Dymond was responsible for its classic design

but died aged 38 at the initial planning stage. Charles Fowler completed the assignment, adding this to an impressive line of architectural achievements which included Totnes Bridge and Covent Garden. This market was known locally as the Eastern Market whereas the Lower Market, nearer Fore Street, was the Western Market.

There are thirteen clock towers in Devon and none finer than the grand specimen at the end of Exeter's Queen Street. The tower was erected to the memory of William Miles by his wife. He was a well known philanthropist and animal lover so drinking troughs were located on all four corners. The opening ceremony was a graceful and dignified affair with Mrs Miles arriving in a carriage pulled by two magnificent grey horses. Most local residents simply refer to it as The Clocktower. This is less of a mouthful than its original title The Miles Memorial Clock and Drinking Fountain. Since its erection in 1897, it has witnessed a growing amount of traffic around its base. In fact the volume of traffic along New North Road has almost resulted in the tower being dismantled. Fortunately not many horses, sheep or cattle add to the chaos by passing this way today!

The beauty of Exeter is greatly enhanced by its floral displays. All around the city, from roundabouts to window boxes, and from flower borders to the many parks and gardens, Exeter is a place of floral animation. This has not gone unnoticed; the city has won many national trophies and in 1981-82 won the title of European Floral City.

The plants which decorate so many parts of the city are nurtured at Belle Isle, formerly a sewage works, down by the River Exe. The garden staff pioneered the technique of growing petunias in gro-bags and should be congratulated for their marvellous efforts as the city centre has blossomed into a colourful and attractive environment.

The little church of St Pancras stands as a fine reminder of old Exeter, its old neighbours having been either blitzed or demolished. It once stood in a shady little lane called Waterbeer Street, not far from Exeter's police station, a drab and dreary place. Beside it stood an even seedier snooker hall, so smoke-ridden that it was almost impossible to see across the room.

St Pancras is one of the oldest churches in the city, its font may well be pre-Norman. For many years, up to 1889, it stood derelict but Mr J L Pearson restored it and it became quite fashionable for the Mayor to adopt it as his Parish Church, in State, on one Sunday each year. Earlier this century anyone wishing to view it had to apply to Mr Algar, an ironmonger from Waterbeer Street. Today the church is surrounded by concrete and glass, and the odd peculiar sculpture, and is freely open to everyone.

Gandy Street is a revitalised street; at one time it was a dismal backstreet with little going for it as a commercial trading area apart from wine bars and art centres. A great deal of enthusiasm has seen this dingy road transformed into a thriving thorough-

Gandy Street

fare with some upmarket attractions to catch the eye.

The street was originally called Currestreet or Curry Street, which possibly meant Dog Street, or the street where the leather workers carried on their trade. The latter derivation is the one preferred, but in the early eighteenth century it changed its name to Gandy Lane after a local family. Other theories suggest that in the seventeenth century this road was called St Lucie's Lane, but I have seen no cartographical proof.

Rougemont Gardens are lovely grounds which run into Northernhay Park and are the perfect place to relax away from the hustle and bustle of city centre life. Less than a 100 yards from the High Street, and tucked between the library, the Castle and the city wall, they are a popular choice with office and shop workers whilst young couples will often be seen happily entwined in some quiet hollow. Please do not disturb!

This parkland haven in central Exeter was once private gardens and prior to April 1912, when they became public, visitors could only enjoy them on Thursdays. The owner, Miss Outhwaite, opened them just one day each week, and then anybody who wanted to view them was obliged to leave their calling card at the door beforehand!

The house that went with the grounds was originally built in 1774, by John Patch, on land leased from the Duchy of Cornwall, but the building we see today, near the main entrance, was an enlarged version built by Edmund Granger, a wealthy wool merchant, in 1787.

The setting for the house and grounds is an old volcanic stump, 'rouge' indicating a certain redness in the rock and the 'mont' revealing the hilly aspect of this location. The stone from Rougemont has been much used in the past for local buildings and its presence can be easily detected in the city wall.

The great dip at Rougemont is part of the works prescribed by William the Conqueror in 1068 and was known then as Exeter Castle. It was built on a space which was previously open on its upper plateau but colonised by many little houses on its slopes. After 1068 the great ditch could only be crossed by a drawbridge making it a fine stronghold. The Castle had its moments of glory and high drama, withstanding at least eight sieges but eventually fell into decay and by 1669 was almost ruinous.

The Castle and side entrance to Rougemont Gardens

The gardens though are still in great shape and those with an interest in plants and trees will have a 'field day' exploring the grounds. The un-initiated enthusiast will be able to read the botanical names of each speci-man as the trees are labelled. Amongst the wide range of exotic trees you will find the Judas Tree, the Strawberry Tree, the Maidenhair Tree and Medlar trees. A first class leaflet which describes a Tree Walk through these gardens unearths this wondrous gem of information: apparently the fruit of the medlar was highly popular in the medieval period, it is picked in autumn time and is only worth consuming when in a semi-rotten state.

A short distance from the High Street, reached by passing through the old,

low arch of St Stephen's Bow, is a complex of ruins. These are the remains
of St Katherine's Almshouses with its ruined little chapel in its midst.
These were founded by Canon John Stevens in 1457 and demolished by German
bombers in 1942. The chapel, now roofless, had a fine wagen roof and a
tesselated Roman pavement was discovered on this site by a Mr Everett.

The adjacent area around Bedford Street was particularly badly hit by the
air raids, the number of new buildings in the district being evidence of
this.

The board outside the Ship Inn in Martins Lane proudly proclaims the fact
that the legendary Sir Francis Drake was an enthusiastic patron of this old
inn. It claims Sir Francis wrote "Next to my own ship I do most love that
old Ship in Exon, a tavern in Fish Street, as the people call it, or as the
clergy will have it, St Martins Lane." (This, of course, is the modern
translation!) He continues by recounting his next day's task of returning to
Plymouth in order to prepare for his encounter with the Spanish Armada. The
rest is history!

Rumour has it that he was occasionally prone to quaff more ale than was
good for him and that he was ejected from the pub for raucous behaviour.

Like all good old pubs it is said to be haunted and an Exeter lady called
Mrs Gill, who once worked there, claims to have been pushed down a flight of
steps by the ghost.

In 1710 an angry mob tried to burn down this inn. They thought that some
whig-sponsored clergy were being sheltered there. Fortunately a group of
soldiers doused the fire - and almost put an end to the rioters as well.

Newbridge Street and Fore Street is where Exeter's city centre begins or
ends, a thoroughfare incorporating a variety of shops far greater than any
other street in Exeter - avenues of individuality in a consumer world of
chain store city centre domination.

Bridge Street was first forged as a route to a new bridge which was opened
in 1778. Fore Street, meaning 'the street before the main street', leads to

The Ship Inn in Martin's Lane

the High Street. In some ways these two streets are depressing with their incessant traffic and drab buildings, and are certainly not colourful or inviting streets at first glance. However a more careful and thoughtful study will reveal a place of great character, with many small and large shops offering personal service when buying anything from a pair of thermal Long Johns to something much more erotic.

To give a precise portrayal of all Fore Street's undoubted parts and attractions would be courting folly as it sees so many changes. However, amongst its permanent features are Tuckers' Hall and St Nicholas Priory, which lies a short distance from Fore Street along the lane, refreshingly called the Mint.

Tuckers' Hall was built as a meeting place where the Corporation of Weavers, Fullers and Shearmen could discuss business. Exeter at one time was an important centre for the production of woollen goods. Most people appreciate what weavers and shearmen did but fullers perhaps need some clarification. Fullers (also known as tuckers) had the difficult task of removing the grease from the wool and the fulling mills, not far away close to the River

Exe, removed the lanolin in the wool. As people often took their names from their occupations it will come as no surpise to learn that, in this area, there are many Tuckers and Fullers listed in the telephone directory.

Originally St Nicholas Priory was a Benedictine Priory and it has been estimated that what is left is only about a quarter of the original. It was founded by William Rufus on land which William the Conqueror had granted to the monks of Battle Abbey, together with the nearby church of St Olave. The vaulted cellar has impressively thick Norman pillars and the ribs of the vaulting are of an interesting character. In its early days it was believed that it was a place where miracles happened. This assured its prosperity as visiting pilgrims generously supported the establishment.

In 1102 the Priory was guilty of over enthusiastic bell ringing, which upset Bishop Osbern. The camponoligical conflict was resolved by the Archdeacon. Three centuries later a dispute went to a far higher court, the Pope. This was over whether or not dead monks could be buried in their own cemetery. It was resolved in favour of the monks who were allowed to continue in the habit of burying their own dead.

In 1535 commissioners ordered the breakers to begin demolition of St Nicholas Priory starting with the rood loft. Then they went off for dinner. Meanwhile a determined band of ladies arrived armed with spikes, shovels, pikes and any other tools they could lay hands on and broke open the church door. They shouted at the man knocking down the rood loft, bombarded him with stones and, brandishing their pikes etc, chased him up to the tower. The poor man leapt out of a window, breaking a rib in the process. Alderman John Blackaller hurried up to stop the riot with fair words or foul. One lady gave him a blow and sent him packing but the women were seized and taken to prison. Meanwhile the commissioners, still at dinner, were hastily summoned and, fortunately for the women, they tempered justice with mercy and ordered their release.

After the Dissolution the buildings and other encumbrances were sold off and various people acquired property there. The City Council paid £850 for it in 1913 and began restoring it. Harold Brakspear masterminded the work, a person extremely talented in the field of ecclesiastical architecture. Today it is a small museum well worthy of a visit.

As far as most Exonians are concerned, Cornish's is not just an outfitters store but more a local institution, as for over the last century thousands of people have been kitted out by this firm.

The company claims the unique distinction of having been located on six different corner sites in Exeter at various times. They started out at Eastgate Corner in April 1884, were at Broadgate Corner for a while, and

eventually reached their present location in 1905.
  Cornish's building is a distinctive landmark, its unusual turret and
flagpole making it clearly identifiable from well outside the outskirts of

the city. By the same token, the view from it is most impressive but only
privy to its workforce and special guests.
  Originally the building, which still bears the name Paternoster House, was

built as a paper store for the local printing firm of Wheaton's, therefore its floors and walls were built to support immense weights making it fortress-like in strength.

On the same site, years earlier, stood an ironmonger's shop which was owned by a gentleman who put his trust in divine providence rather than a provident insurance company. He was the only trader, in the block of buildings which made the L-shape around the corner of North and Fore Streets, not to be insured, claiming that God would provide. Amazingly, after an immense fire razed all the other buildings to the ground, his business stood intact and relatively unscathed. The building was taken down when the entire site was redeveloped, without financial loss to him.

To entice more distant clientele, in 1920 Cornish's placed an advertisement in the local press with the promise that any persons travelling to Exeter, from within a radius of twenty-five miles, could, if they bought garments to the value of £2 or more, claim a refund of half the railway fare, on displaying the return half of the ticket.

The electric lift was not installed until 1934, thus making interdepartmental trips easier, especially for shopppers, who had a guide to show them to the right department. This was the first lift to be installed in Exeter and, despite its various ups and downs, gave excellent service until it was eventually replaced by a more modern Otis lift.

Although Cornish's was taken over in 1981 it still remains a family business, a rarity in these days of High Street chain store shops.

Cornish's is located on a formerly important junction which was known as the 'Carfax'. This word originated from the French 'carreforc' meaning crossroads or from the Latin 'quadri-furcus' meaninq four forking roads! Being such a focal point in the past meant that a lot of traffic passed by on the four major routes into the City.

Unfortunately for several centuries the progress of traffic was hindered by the Great Conduit which was sited near the junction. It was pulled down and rebuilt on a number of occasions, usually because it was blocking the road. Obviously water was a very important commodity in a town where timber was a key material of most buildings. The city scavengers of the sixteenth century had the task of checking that every man had a vessel of water at his door throughout the summertime, in case of fire.

The conduit in lower South Gate Street wasn't supplied from the Underground Passages and may have got its water from the spring in the garden of the Bishop's Palace. This water acquired a considerable reputation as being excellent for making tea at a time when this beverage was becoming fashionable.

ALONG THE WATERFRONT

Exeter grew into an important location mainly because it was at a point on the River Exe where the river could be forded at low tide. Between the position of the present Exe Bridges and the sea at Exmouth, there was no other point where it was possible to wade across.

Exeter has a long waterfront which stretches from Cowley Bridge, a few miles north of the Exe Bridges, right the way down to Topsham, one of Devon's most sought after residential settlements. It is possible to walk long stretches beside the river or canal, although most people settle for a gentle stroll along short sections. To accompany your wanderings, here are stories, facts, observations and opinions of just some of the places along the route.

The waterside area from above St David's railway station towards Exe Bridges, has necessarily seen vast changes in recent decades. After many years of floods in the flatlands beside the Exe, various flood prevention schemes have alleviated the watery problem. The great concrete dykes accept the overflow waters but unfortunately the scene looks sterile and could be enhanced by landscaping to create a more rural feel to the surroundings.

The two weirs beside the 'Mill on the Exe' public house are called Head Weir and Blackaller Weir. The former created a head of water for a series of leats that drained Exe Island, and provided the flow for a great number of waterwheels on land between the City wall and the River Exe - a medieval industrial estate no less!

Blackaller Weir and The Mill on the Exe

Above Head Weir people once swam in the River Exe, a spartan activity done within the confines of a roped off area. There were even changing rooms, on the east bank, but the advent of swimming pools provided a more attractive and safer option. The river was certainly cleaner and the summers must have been better at the turn of the century!

It is possible that many of those bathers were workers at the mill by the Exe when it was a working paper mill. The site was cleared to make way for the pub and, on a fine day, provides a splendid beer garden in which to watch canoeists, fishermen and other people enjoying themselves in, on or by the river. Just around a bend in the river are the Exe Bridges.

Exe Bridges have always been synonomous with traffic jams, and no Exonian happily anticipates undertaking a journey across them at peak times - a situation not improved now by an excessive number of traffic lights.

Close to the current bridges is part of the remains of the first stone bridge to span the Exe, a much larger construction as the river was much wider, although shallower, centuries ago. An eighteen-arched bridge was

built about 1258, designed by Exeter's mayor at that time, Walter Gervase, who had witnessed many drownings at the dangerous ford. He also gave a big donation towards the cost of construction. Unfortunately Walter died in 1259. A skeleton found buried in the bridge, when most of it was dismantled in 1883, is believed to have been his.

It seems that there was a hermit in the thirteenth century who built herself a hut on the stone bridge over the Exe and there, plumb in the middle of the traffic, refused to budge. Traffic, and therefore trade, was totally obstructed and complaints were aimed at the justices by the city fathers but nothing was done to remove her, and so five years on she was still there. And motorists today think they have it bad!

In 1539 disaster struck this bridge when one of its central arches collapsed. Mr Edward Bridgeman (appropriately named!) who bought a quantity of stones from the recently demolished St Nicholas Church, used these to repair the bridge. An ancient prophecy was thus fulfilled because, centuries earlier, it had been predicted that the waters of the Exe would flow beneath this church.

Further bridges, to accommodate greater flows of traffic, were built in 1778 and 1905 but the present constructions are much more recent and, judging by popular opinion, no better for the job! One solution, considering the layout of the city, is another road bridge spanning the Exe about half way between Exe Bridges and Countess Wear, a suggestion made some forty years ago.

Beside the Exe Bridges and the Quay, on the city bank, is an area of new housing which occupies the Shilhay, an area which has seen drastic changes

in recent years.

   At one time the Shilhay was the industrial heartland of Exeter. There were many factories and businesses, its main thoroughfare being aptly called Commercial Road. The firm J L Thomas made candles and soap whilst Tremletts carried on a tannery trade, beating hides and skin. Maggots and rats were side products in a district which was generally dreary and depressing to see. The demise of canal trade and the growth of the Marsh Barton Trading Estate, turned this area into a twilight zone prime for redevelopment.

Some of the well built bonded warehouses were converted into night clubs; Tiffany's and The Quay Club occupy the premises of a former whisky distillery.

In recent years Exeter's quayside area has witnessed a vast number of changes aimed at recreating a maritime atmosphere and you can judge for yourself whether or not this has succeeded. Certainly this part of the waterfront is more lively than it was twenty-five years ago, with people being drawn to its nightspots, bars, river activities, riverside walks and, of course, the Maritime Museum.

The handsome Custom House is a reflection of Exeter's former maritime trade and importance and was built in 1681, making it one of the earliest brick buildings in the city. Originally it had an open arcade so that goods brought ashore could be stowed away with ease. An increase in trading meant that more space within the building was necessary and the arches were filled in. John Abbot, of Frithelstock in West Devon, was paid the princely sum of £35 to create its wonderfully ornate plaster ceilings, a feature which will impress its visitors. Another feature is the 'Queen's Pipe' where illicitly imported or smuggled tobacco was burnt off. Measuring equipment and other related items of customs work may be seen.

In front of the Custom House are two cannons complete with gun carriages, an innocent enough ornament to set off the building's fine frontage. However, these impressive guns have their own history. They were originally fashioned in Scotland as part of an order made by the Russians but, when they became surplus to requirements, a new use was found - to be placed at the foot of the Wellington Monument on the Blackdown Hills in Somerset. Sixteen of these cannons reached Exeter Quay in 1819 but alas the funds ran out and, as the various landing dues could not be met, they were impounded. Although some lay redundant in storage two served a useful purpose - acting as bollards on the quayside. When the Quay area was reshaped in 1983 they were restored and mounted on their carriages. And the Wellington monument has at last received a couple - although they had to wait a century and a half for them!

Just beneath the City Wall is a small building with a neat Dutch gable. This was once the wharfinger's office and dates back to 1778, a handy location for managing the trade of Exeter Quay and equally well sited to keep tabs on the tides and affairs of Exeter's International Maritime Museum.

If all the efforts of man (roads, buildings etc.) were removed from Exeter's Quay, the scene revealed would be a line of steep, red sandstone cliffs rising from a flat, low sandstone shelf of rock. This natural landing place was adapted as such in 1564, the same year that John Trew was engineering the first Exeter Canal. The old warehouses which lie between the former wharfinger's office and the Prospect Inn are believed to be the oldest known warehouses of their type, in England, still in existence. Their massive beams extended out over the water and permitted vessels to be unloaded under cover. Modern excavations have unearthed the remains of a Tudor Quay at a lower level.

The Prospect Inn occupies a site which has boasted an inn for more than two centuries.

However the present building dates back to the nineteenth century and was originally called The Fountain Inn. The Prospect has absorbed the adjacent building, Rose Cottage, as part of its premises. In 1955 this inn enjoyed much publicity when it was the prize for a competition run by the Daily Sketch. (Exeter's pubs seem to appeal to the 'Nationals', as The Heart of Oak in Pinhoe was similarly a prize in the Sun newspaper in 1986.)

The boat apparently left high and dry opposite the Prospect Inn was presented by the Tyne Lifeboat Society, a forerunner of the RNLI. It was built in 1886 and served forty-four years, averaging just over one rescue launch per year, until it was taken out of commission in 1930. Without doubt it saved many lives and now lives a quiet, well deserved retirement beneath the old fish market on the Quay.

One of the Quay's 'finest hours' must have been when it was the centre of attention during the filming of the BBC's 'Onedin Line' series (not that it was playing itself in the programme - it was meant to be Liverpool!) However, this attention might well have sparked off the idea to develop the Quay as a conservation area and tourist attraction.

The tallest warehouses along the Quay have enjoyed fluctuating fortunes since their erection in 1835. One is principally formed of limestone, rock which was probably brought around the coastline from Torquay and Berry Head. At these coastal locations the stone was hewn straight from the towering seacliffs onto vessels for immediate delivery to Exeter.

These warehouses are built into a natural cliff and it has been rumoured that secret tunnels, used by smugglers, led from them to the basements of buildings in the Georgian Colleton Crescent above. A raised ledge, further along the Quay, was used by Custom and Excise men to watch out for any such irregularities.

The ferry which traverses the Exe to the Marsh Barton bank of the river is a long established one, dating back to 1750. It is one of the only manual ferries in Europe to operate on a chain, which proved useful at times in the past when one drunken ferryman needed the chain to keep from drifting merrily down the river.

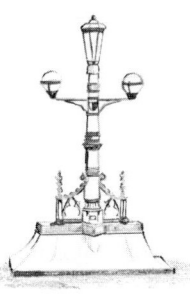

The unusual lamps either side of the ferry were manufactured in Scotland by W Macfarlane and Co of Glasgow. There were originally six of them which stood on a former Exe Bridge (the one which was opened in 1905 and dismantled in 1973). The lamps lay dormant until 1983 when they were restored and resited on Exeter Quay as part of the Conservation scheme. They possess a part of the city coat of arms and are painted in the city's official colours of green.

Downstream from the Quay vehicular access ceases and pedestrian exploration prevails, and it is a very popular venue for dog walkers. About a quarter of a mile below the Quay is The Port Royal Inn, a popular port of call which was once hit by a freak tornado.

The Port Royal Inn with the distinctive spire of St Leonard's Church behind

Nearby is Trew's Weir, built in the 1560s to give a head of water for the first Exeter Canal, possibly the first canal to be built in England. However it was a Welshman who engineered it. This was John Trew who signed a contract which waived any fee for his work if ten-ton tub boats could not use his canal at all stages of the tide. They couldn't. So the poor fellow wasn't paid for his labours.

Trew's Canal only went as far as Countess Wear, one and three quarters of a mile downstream, where vessels rejoined the river below the weir placed across it in 1282 by Lady Isabella de Fortibus, Countess of Devon, Lady of the Isle of Wight (all one and the same person!)

Trew's Weir Mill lies in a sadly derelict state. It was built in 1780 and fifteen years later it was recorded as a cotton spinning mill (the cotton spun - not the mill) where 300 people were employed. It became a paper mill in 1834 and many extensions were added. At one time it had the contract to provide paper for the manufacture of tickets for the London Underground.

Part of the strange complex of buildings which extend from Trew's Weir Mills is a conglomeration known locally as The Match Factory. This name is

Trew's Weir Mills

*mysteriously and mistakenly used, for matches were never manufactured or
even stored there. However, it is possible that a form of 'slow match' may
have been made there. This would have been an impregnated cotton strip, the
cotton coming from the nearby mill, used for lighting the fuse to fire cannons. The oldest part of the decaying buildings dates back to 1774 and
around the 1850s it was shown on maps as Lower Mill. Flax was produced there*

Trew's Weir

and troughs where the non-fibrous elements were removed may be seen if the undergrowth permits. Other past uses include that of a bag manufacturing centre, a stable and a warehouse although rumour has it that theatrical shows or plays have also, occasionally, been staged there.

The wayfarer may continue on along the riverside path to Salmon Pool, and beyond along St James' Leat to Countess Weir, a pleasant enough romp away from the noise and bustle of traffic.

An alternative route lies across the nearby suspension bridge which, when put into motion by over enthusiastic joggers, causes a quite sickening sensation. It was built in the 1930s to provide a short cut for the large workforce at Willeys, the iron founders, to ease their journeys to and from work.

The path leads to the Exeter Canal, the final version engineered by the distinguished engineer James Green in 1827. A pleasant ramble of just over a mile leads to the Double Locks Hotel, built in 1702 and believed to be the oldest inn beside a canal in England. The building exists thanks to Exeter's past sea trade with Holland. Bricks, called 'clinkers', were brought back as ballast - these being used to build The Locks (the pub not the gates). It has a lovely beer garden, with a barbeque area in the grounds. Its location and atmosphere have made it a firm favourite with young people, a perfect place to spend a summer evening.

At the northern end of the canal is the Canal Basin added, again by James Green, in 1830 and originally called The New Cut on old maps. Today the main part of Exeter's Maritime Museum is housed there, a wonderful collection of ships, boats and maritime vessels of all shapes and sizes. ISCA (The International Sailing Craft Association) manage the collection which has been assembled from all corners of the globe.

And Finally ...

We have now reached the end of our brief look at Exeter, 'brief' being the operative word. No doubt the historical purists and literary pedants could find fault and complain that the detail is not sufficiently deep. However, that was never the aim of this book; we set out to produce a highly visual book, seasoned with stories and spiced up with odd little anecdotes.

In putting the book together many sources and people were consulted. There were often contradictions and conflicting facts to sort out, for example the true origin of the cannons outside the custom house, or the number of arches in the first stone Exe Bridge, and the spelling of the 'Carfax' and so on. These issues provided much headscratching but the most popular version in each case has been chosen. However, no publication is without fault or inaccuracy, and we don't expect this one to be either.

If your appetite has been whetted for more knowledge, and you enjoyed the lighthearted approach to the subjects, my other book on Exeter, The Lost City of Exeter, does cover some of the same ground but deals with the subjects in greater depth and also covers a whole range of different aspects - the sport and entertainment, disappearing villages etc. Also, the libraries have shelves full of books on the many different aspects of this ancient city and if any particular subject appeals to you, it shouldn't be too difficult to follow it up for more information.

It has been fun compiling this little book and we hope you will have fun reading it - and find it to be both informative and entertaining.

Jane Reynolds trained at Exeter College of Art in Graphic Design and Illustration. She is married to Ken Leonard, they have two children and live in Cullompton. This is the second book consisting entirely of her illustrations, and she has illustrated all the other 'Obelisk' titles.

Chips Barber is a teacher in Exeter, and devotes his spare time to writing and publishing local books. The rest of his spare time is spent teaching evening classes and keep-fit sessions, giving illustrated talks, after-dinner speeches and leading guided walks, and in his spare time he runs a Dartmoor walking club. If he had any other spare time he would like to support Exeter City, play golf and snooker and go fishing.

Sally Barber is Chips' better half, the nine-tenths of the iceberg that isn't seen, who divides her time between the home and publishing business for a fraction of the acclaim - and that just about sums it up!

If you have enjoyed reading this book, you may like to read one of Chips Barber's other books:

The Great Little Dartmoor Book
The Lost City of Exeter
The Torbay Book
Diary of a Dartmoor Walker
Diary of a Devonshire Walker
The DevonAir Book of Family Walks

Also, by other authors:

Adventure Through Red Devon, *Raymond B Cattell*
Under Sail through South Devon & Dartmoor, *R B Cattell*
An Exeter Boyhood, *Frank Retter*
Ide, *Bill Rowland*
Rambling in the Plymouth Countryside, *D Woolley & M Lister*
Great Walks of Dartmoor, *Terry Bound*
Tales of the Unexplained in Devon, *Judy Chard*

If you have difficulty in obtaining any of these books, please write to Obelisk Publications, 2 Church Hill, Pinhoe, Exeter or telephone Exeter 68556 for an up-to-date price list. We will post any book(s) free of charge. Chips will autograph any of his books.

First published in 1987
by Obelisk Publications
2 Church Hill, Pinhoe, Exeter, Devon
Designed by Chips, typeset by Sally Barber
Printed in Great Britain by Penwell Ltd
Parkwood, Callington, Cornwall